M000086592

DATE DUE

Demco, Inc. 38-293

MOORE MIDDLE SCHOOL LMC

BC 21030

MATHWORKS!

Using Math to

Design a
ROLLER COASTER

by Hilary Koll, Steve Mills,
and Korey T. Kiepert

Math and Curriculum Consultant:
Debra Voege, Science and Math
Curriculum Resource Teacher

GARETH STEVENS
GS
PUBLISHING
A Member of the WRC Media Family of Companies

MOORE MIDDLE SCHOOL LMC

Please visit our web site at: **www.garethstevens.com**
For a free color catalog describing Gareth Stevens Publishing's
list of high-quality books and multimedia programs, call
1-800-542-2595 (USA) or 1-800-387-3178 (Canada).
Gareth Stevens Publishing's fax: (414) 332-3567.

Library of Congress Cataloging-in-Publication Data

Koll, Hilary.
    Using math to design a roller coaster / Hilary Koll, Steve Mills,
and Korey T. Kiepert. — North American ed.
        p. cm. — (Mathworks!)
    ISBN-10: 0-8368-6766-1 — ISBN-13: 978-0-8368-6766-4 (lib. bdg.)
    ISBN-10: 0-8368-6773-4 — ISBN-13: 978-0-8368-6773-2 (softcover)
    1. Mathematics—Problems, exercises, etc.—Juvenile literature.
    2. Roller coasters—Design and construction–Juvenile literature.
    I. Mills, Steve, 1955- II. Kiepert, Korey T. III. Title. IV. Series.
    QA43.K624   2006
    510.76—dc22   2006040565

This North American edition first published in 2007 by
Gareth Stevens Publishing
A Member of the WRC Media Family of Companies
330 West Olive Street, Suite 100
Milwaukee, Wisconsin 53212 USA

This U.S. edition copyright © 2007 by Gareth Stevens, Inc.
Original edition copyright © 2006 by ticktock Entertainment
Ltd. First published in Great Britain in 2006 by ticktock Media
Ltd., Unit 2, Orchard Business Centre, North Farm Road,
Tunbridge Wells, Kent, TN2 3XF, United Kingdom.

Technical Consultant: Korey T. Kiepert
Korey has a degree in Mechanical Engineering from Michigan
Technological University. He works for The Gravity Group, a
firm that specializes in designing wooden roller coasters,
including The Voyage and Hades.

Gareth Stevens editor: Dorothy L. Gibbs
Gareth Stevens Art Direction: Tammy West

Photo credits (t=top, b=bottom, c=center, l=left, r=right)
Cedar Point: 1, 14-15, 18-19, 29l. Gravity Group: 2-3, 4-5, 6-7,
8-9, 10-11, 12-13, 16-17, 20-21, 22-23, 24-25, 26-27, 29c.

Every effort has been made to trace the copyright holders
for the photos used in this book. The publisher apologizes,
in advance, for any unintentional omissions and would be
pleased to insert the appropriate acknowledgements in
any subsequent edition of this publication.

All rights reserved to Gareth Stevens, Inc. No part of
this book may be reproduced, stored in a retrieval system,
or transmitted in any form or by any means, electronic,
mechanical, photocopying, recording, or otherwise, without
the prior written permission of the publisher.

Printed in the United States of America

1 2 3 4 5 6 7 8 9 10 09 08 07 06

CONTENTS

HAVE FUN WITH MATH (How to Use This Book)   4

KNOW YOUR COASTERS   6

CHOOSE A BUILDING PLOT   8

HOW ROLLER COASTERS WORK   10

COASTER DESIGNS   12

TWISTS, TURNS, AND HILLS   14

LOOPS AND TUNNELS   16

PASSENGERS   18

ORDERING MATERIALS   20

BUILDING THE COASTER   22

TESTING AND TRIAL RUNS   24

READY TO ROLL!   26

MATH TIPS   28

ANSWERS   30

GLOSSARY/MEASUREMENT CONVERSIONS   32

HAVE FUN WITH MATH

How to Use This Book

Math is important in the daily lives of people everywhere. We use math when we play games, ride bicycles, or go shopping, and everyone uses math at work. Imagine you have been hired to design and build a roller coaster! You may not realize it, but engineers use math for everything from drawing up plans to inspecting structures for safety. In this book, you will be able to try lots of exciting math activities, using real-life data and facts about roller coasters. If you can work with numbers, measurements, shapes, charts, and diagrams, then you could DESIGN A ROLLER COASTER.

How does it feel to design a thrill ride?

Grab your plot map and find out what it takes to make a bigger and better roller coaster.

Math Activities

The coaster clipboards have math activities for you to try. Get your pencil, ruler, and notebook (for figuring out problems and listing answers).

BUILDING THE COASTER

The materials have arrived. Now you must start the difficult work of building the roller coaster. You will need lots of workers to construct the hills and tunnels. You will also need skilled people to set up the support structures and to lay the tracks. You must plan the timing of the construction work carefully. A medium-sized wooden roller coaster takes about nine months to build. Because most amusement parks are open only during summer, you have the winter months to build the ride, but this time frame often means building in cold, wet weather.

Coaster Work

The DATA BOX on page 23 contains information about how long each part of the building work might take. Use this information to help you estimate the number of weeks it could take to complete all the jobs.

Be careful. Some time spans are given in weeks, and some are given in months. To convert weeks to months or months to weeks, think of one month as four weeks.

22

NEED HELP?

- If you are not sure how to do some of the math problems, turn to pages 28 and 29, where you will find lots of tips to help get you started.

- Turn to pages 30 and 31 to check your answers.
(Try all the activities and challenges before you look at the answers.)

- Turn to page 32 for definitions of some words and terms used in this book.

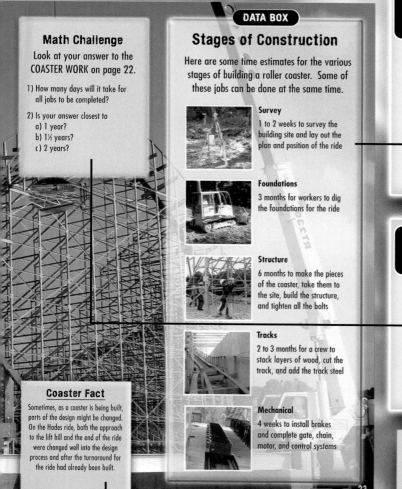

Math Challenge

Look at your answer to the COASTER WORK on page 22.

1) How many days will it take for all jobs to be completed?

2) Is your answer closest to
a) 1 year?
b) 1½ years?
c) 2 years?

DATA BOX

Stages of Construction

Here are some time estimates for the various stages of building a roller coaster. Some of these jobs can be done at the same time.

Survey
1 to 2 weeks to survey the building site and lay out the plan and position of the ride

Foundations
3 months for workers to dig the foundations for the ride

Structure
6 months to make the pieces of the coaster, take them to the site, build the structure, and tighten all the bolts

Tracks
2 to 3 months for a crew to stack layers of wood, cut the track, and add the track steel

Mechanical
4 weeks to install brakes and complete gate, chain, motor, and control systems

Coaster Fact

Sometimes, as a coaster is being built, parts of the design might be changed. On the Hades ride, both the approach to the lift hill and the end of the ride were changed well into the design process and after the turnaround for the ride had already been built.

23

Math Facts and Data

To complete some of the math activities, you will need information from a DATA BOX, which looks like this.

Math Challenge

Blue boxes, like this one, have extra math questions to challenge you. Give them a try!

You will find lots of amazing details about roller coasters in FACT boxes that look like this.

How much do you know about roller coasters? Do you know how high some of the tallest coasters are? Do you know which of the world's roller coasters give the longest rides? Which are fastest? Which roller coasters carry the most people? Which are considered the most exciting? You will need to know all these facts to design a roller coaster that is bigger and better than the rest. There are two different types of roller coasters: coasters made with steel tracks and coasters made with wooden tracks. A wooden coaster has tracks made of wood, but the structure can be made of steel or wood.

Coaster Work

In the DATA BOX on page 7, you will see a table showing information about roller coasters around the world. Use the information in the table to help you answer these questions.

1) Which roller coaster is
   a) the highest?
   b) the fastest?
   c) the longest?
   d) the oldest?

2) How much taller is
   a) Kingda Ka than The Beast?
   b) Top Thrill Dragster than Daidarasaurus?
   c) Tower of Terror than The Voyage?

3) One coaster travels twice as fast as another coaster. Which two coasters are they?

4) How many years between the opening of
   a) Dodonpa and The Voyage?
   b) The Ultimate and The Beast?
   c) The Big Dipper and Hades?

Coaster History Facts

- Russian ice slides were the earliest roller coasters. People sat in carved-out blocks of ice and rode down wooden slides.
- In the 1800s, a railroad was built in the United States to take coal downhill to a river. In the 1870s, the railroad was no longer being used for coal so people rode the train down the hillside.
- The first real roller coaster opened in 1884 at Coney Island in New York. It was called the Switchback Railway.
- By 1930, the United States alone had two thousand roller coasters.

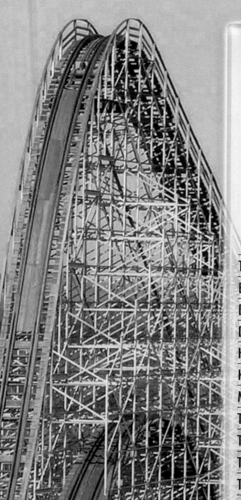

Highest, Fastest, and Longest Coasters

Here is a list of some of the highest, fastest, and longest roller coasters in the world.

The coasters with steel tracks are marked (S).
The coasters with wooden tracks are marked (W).

	height (feet)	top speed (miles per hour)	length (feet)	year open
The Beast (W) — Ohio, USA	112	65	7,402	1979
Big Dipper (W) — Blackpool, UK	59	42	3,297	1923
Daidarasaurus (S) — Japan	92	45	7,677	1970
Dodonpa (S) — Japan	171	107	3,900	2001
Hades (W) — Wisconsin, USA	138	65	4,728	2005
Kingda Ka (S) — New Jersey, USA	456	128	3,117	2005
Millennium Force (S) — Ohio, USA	299	92	6,594	2000
Top Thrill Dragster (S) — Ohio, USA	420	120	2,799	2003
Tower of Terror (S) — Australia	377	100	1,234	1997
The Ultimate (S) — Lightwater Valley, UK	105	50	7,448	1991
The Voyage (W) — Indiana, USA	161	67	6,444	2006

The roller coaster Hades opened at the Mt. Olympus theme park in Wisconsin in 2005.

Math Challenge

Look at the information in the DATA BOX on this page.

1) Put the list in order of each coaster's top speed, from fastest to slowest.

2) How many coasters have a top speed
   a) greater than Hades?
   b) the same as Hades?
   c) less than Hades?

Before designing your roller coaster, you must decide the size and shape of the plot of land you will build it on. Sometimes, new roller coasters have to fit in between other rides at a theme park, or you might have a lake, a tree, a building, or some other object that cannot be moved in the middle of your plot of land. After you have chosen a plot of land, you will know better how to design your coaster. Keep in mind that what makes roller coasters exciting are the unexpected turns, drops, and high hills that make passengers feel as if they are speeding out of control.

Coaster Work

In the DATA BOX on page 9, you will see coordinate grids for different plots of land. Look closely at each grid to answer these questions.

1) Which plot of land, A, B, C, or D, has
   a) a tree at coordinates (3, 1)?
   b) a lake at coordinates (2, 5)?
   c) other rides at coordinates (5, 3)?
   d) the entrance at coordinates (5, 6)?

2) What are the coordinates of
   a) the tree in plot B?
   b) the lake in plot A?
   c) the entrance in plot D?
   d) the entrance in plot A?

Equipment such as this backhoe is used to clear the land.

Math Challenge

In the DATA BOX on page 9, the area of plot A is 28 squares. Estimate the areas of the other three plots of land?

Plot Facts

Roller coaster designers need to be aware of plot-related planning requirements, such as
• rules that say how far a coaster has to be from the edge of the plot
• restrictions on the height of a coaster
• tests confirming that the ground is solid enough to support the structure

DATA BOX

Plot Choices

The grids below contain plot maps for sites
on which you could build your roller coaster.
Each plot has advantages and disadvantages.

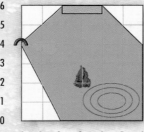

Plot A

This plot has a large mound that could be
used as part of the ride. If you use the
mound, you will not have to construct as high
a hill to still have a big drop, which would
make the coaster less expensive to build.

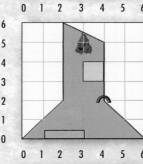

Plot B

This plot is the smallest and has many obstacles
for the ride to avoid, including buildings, another large ride, a lake, and a tree. It does not
have
a natural mound so all hills would have to be
built, increasing the cost of construction.

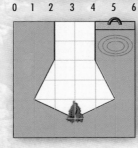

Plot C

This plot is ideal for an out and back, a coaster
that travels out to a point, then turns around
and comes back. An out and back usually has
few twists and turns, but it has lots of hills,
so riders can enjoy plenty of airtime.

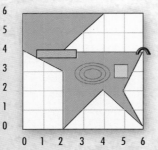

Plot D

This plot has an unusual shape and several
restrictions. The mound is in the center so it
might be difficult to use as part of the coaster,
and the location of the buildings means the
ride would have to go over the top of them.

PLOT KEY

tree   other rides   entrance

mound   buildings   lake

A roller coaster ride is not powered by an engine. The coaster is pulled to the top of a high hill, and gravity takes care of the rest of the ride. The first hill, which is sometimes called the "lift hill," must be the highest hill on the ride. After a coaster speeds down the lift hill, it has the energy to make it up and over the next hill, as long as the next hill is not as high. A roller coaster gradually slows down because of friction inside the wheels. Friction where the wheels touch the track also causes the coaster to slow down a little.

Coaster Work

Remember that a roller coaster's first hill, or "lift hill," must be the highest. Look at the roller coaster designs in the DATA BOX on page 11 to answer the question below.

According to the explanation on this page of how a roller coaster works, which of the designs described in the DATA BOX will work? (Hint: Be sure that the lift hill in each design is the highest hill.)

The lift hill is a roller coaster's highest hill.

Coaster Science

Did you ever notice that when you are going around a turn or a curve in a fast-moving car, your body wants to lean toward the outside of the curve? This happens because of forces that are placed on your body from traveling in a circular motion. The force that is pushing you toward the outside of the curve is called centrifugal force. The faster you go around the curve, the stronger this force will be. Centrifugal force makes roller coasters exciting and fun!

DATA BOX Corkscrews

Some roller coasters have loops, one after another. The loops form twists known as corkscrews.

The information below describes three corkscrews with different numbers of complete turns, or revolutions.

Corkscrew A	2 complete revolutions
Corkscrew B	4 complete revolutions
Corkscrew C	3 complete revolutions

There are 4 right angles in one complete turn, or revolution. A complete revolution is 360°.

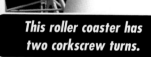

This roller coaster has two corkscrew turns.

Out-and-Back Designs

Many roller coasters have out-and-back designs. These coasters have few twists and turns, but their hills give riders lots of ups and downs and feelings of weightlessness.

Traditional
This out-and-back design takes you straight out and brings you straight back. There are big hills on the way out and small, fast hops on the way back. Because the tracks are close together, they can use the same structure.

start

Double
This design is used to fit an out-and-back ride onto a small building plot. The track goes out and back and then out and back again. The shared structure helps keep the cost of building the ride low.

start

Dog Leg
This out-and-back ride has a bend in the middle and is used to avoid buildings, trees, and other rides.

start

Math Challenge
A full loop, or turn, is 360°.

1) What fraction of a full turn is
   a) 90°?
   b) 180°?
   c) 45°?
   d) 60°?
   e) 30°?
   f) 10°?

2) What are these fractions in their smallest forms?

Put your answers to these questions in a table with three columns.
column 1: Size of turn
column 2: Fraction of a full turn
column 3: Fraction in its smallest form

LOOPS AND TUNNELS

Roller coasters made of steel are better for designs that have complicated loops and turns, especially when they turn riders upside down. All loops have the same basic shape, which looks like an upside-down teardrop. This shape is the most comfortable for riders and helps the roller coaster go faster. A tunnel is another element you might want to add to your coaster design. The noise and darkness inside a tunnel add to a ride's feeling of speed. Sudden drops and changes in direction are scarier in tunnels because riders can't see where they are or what's coming next.

Coaster Work

The drawings below show how to estimate the amount of track needed for a loop. Draw a polygon inside the loop and draw another polygon outside the loop. Find the perimeter of each polygon. The amount of track you need will be a number between the two perimeters.

1) What are the perimeters of the polygons for Loop A?

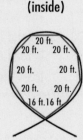

(inside)

(outside)

2) What are the perimeters of the polygons for Loop B?

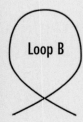

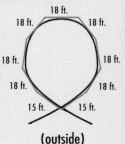

(inside)

(outside)

Loop Facts

- The Flip Flap Railway, built in 1895, was one of the first roller coasters with a loop. Although the ride was popular, it was also dangerous, and it closed after only a few years.
- When Ohio's Son of Beast opened, in 2000, it was the only wooden roller coaster with a loop.

Tunnel Fact

On the Hades coaster, in Wisconsin, riders dive straight into a tunnel after the lift hill. From the top of the lift hill, they look down at a tiny black hole, which gets larger and larger as the coaster speeds toward it. The tunnel runs under a parking lot. The track inside the tunnel has many small hops and turns.

This track is being built inside a tunnel. The cars of the roller coaster will tilt 90° in complete darkness.

Math Challenge

Use the answers to the COASTER WORK questions to find the answer to this question.

If the length of each loop is exactly halfway between the inside and outside perimeters, how long would each loop be?

PASSENGERS

ow you need to think about how many people you want your roller coaster to carry, and you have to decide how long each ride will last. If you want to make money from your roller coaster, you must get as many people as possible to ride on it. If you design a coaster that holds only ten people, and the ride lasts twenty minutes, you will not make much money! Most coasters hold twenty to thirty people, and each ride lasts two to three minutes. You can also have more than one train. While one train is running, the other can be loading or unloading passengers.

Coaster Work

The DATA BOX on page 19 contains a table with information about three roller coaster rides. Use the table to answer these questions.

1) Which ride carries the most people in each train?

2) Which ride lasts the longest?

3) How many rides will run in one hour on
   a) Ride A?
   b) Ride B?
   c) Ride C?

Train Facts

To increase the number of people that can ride on a roller coaster, more than one train can be used. A computerized control system can keep a coaster with more than one train operating safely. A roller coaster ride is split into zones, and the trains have to be separated from each other by at least one zone. The control system keeps a train from entering a zone until that zone is clear.

The Train

A roller coaster train usually has several cars.
Each car might have several benches to sit on.
Each bench usually seats two or three people.
This picture (*right*) shows a train with two
people per bench, two benches per car,
and four cars per train.

A theme park operator wants a new roller coaster.
The coaster designer offers three rides to choose from.

	people per bench	benches per car	cars per train	ride time
Ride A	2	2	6	3 minutes
Ride B	2	3	5	4 minutes
Ride C	3	2	3	2 minutes

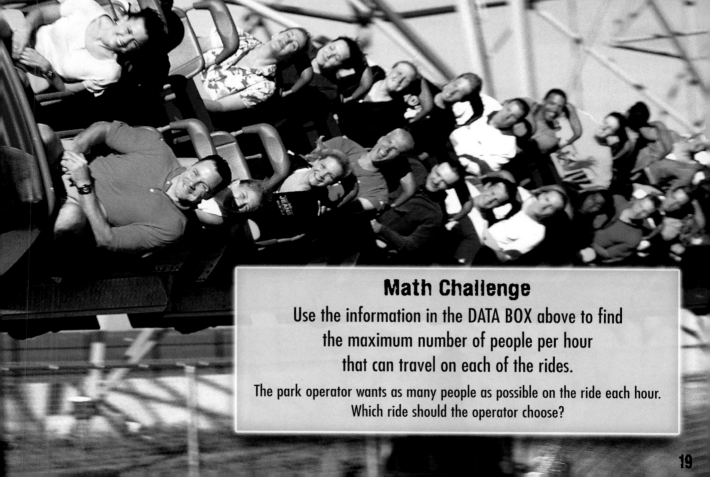

Math Challenge

Use the information in the DATA BOX above to find
the maximum number of people per hour
that can travel on each of the rides.

The park operator wants as many people as possible on the ride each hour.
Which ride should the operator choose?

After you have decided on a roller coaster design and size, you need to order building materials. You will need thousands of steel bars and bolts to construct the ride. The bars are bolted together like a toy construction set. You also have to hire a site overseer to manage the construction of the roller coaster. The site overseer will lease, or rent, all the machines (diggers, cranes, concrete mixers, and so on) needed to build the ride. The structure of the coaster is put together on the ground. Then a crane raises it into place. Your roller coaster is beginning to take shape!

Coaster Work

The DATA BOX on page 21 contains information about materials used to build roller coasters.

1) Write these numbers from the DATA BOX in words.
   a) 141 feet
   b) 170 wooden coasters
   c) 900 legs
   d) 1,200 ribbons
   e) 4,728 feet
   f) 1,882 roller coasters
   g) 1,712 steel coasters
   h) 3,900 items

2) Write the following numbers in figures, or digits.
   a) ninety-three
   b) three hundred eight
   c) seven hundred sixty-four
   d) one thousand four hundred seven
   e) two thousand twenty

Supports called bents hold up a roller coaster. The metal bars used to make the bents are called chords, diagonals, and legs.

DATA BOX

Building Materials

On average, at every 10 feet along a ride, there is a support structure called a bent that holds the track in place. Each bent has 3 legs, 3 chords, 3 diagonals, and 4 ribbons, which are thin, metal bars. A coaster that is 3,000 feet long would need 900 legs, 900 chords, 900 diagonals, and 1,200 ribbons, making a total of 3,900 items — without even including bolts, several other small metal pieces, or the track itself!

The Hades roller coaster is 4,728 feet long, with a drop of 141 feet. About 27,000 pieces of steel, weighing more than 970,000 pounds were used to build this ride. It took 57,000 bolts to join the structure together.

Today, approximately 1,882 roller coasters are operating, worldwide. Of these rides, 1,712 are steel roller coasters, and only 170 are wooden roller coasters.

Math Challenge

For each of the numbers a through g (below), give the value of the bold digit.

Examples: In **4**3, the value of the 4 is forty.
In **2**,300, the value of the 2 is two thousand.

Use these column headings to help you.

HTh	TTh	Th	H	T	U	
	2	7	0	0	0	pieces of steel
	5	7	0	0	0	bolts
9	7	0	0	0	0	pounds

a) **4**,728 feet
b) 1,**8**82 roller coasters
c) 1,**7**12 steel coasters
d) **3**,900 items
e) **2**7,000 pieces of steel
f) **5**7,000 bolts
g) **9**70,000 pounds

Coaster Fact

Roller coaster cars use three types of wheels. Road wheels run on the top of the track. Side wheels, or guide wheels, run along the side of the track. Upstop wheels run on the underside of the track and keep the cars from flying off on hills and drops.

BUILDING THE COASTER

The materials have arrived. Now you must start the difficult work of building the roller coaster. You will need lots of workers to construct the hills and tunnels. You will also need skilled people to set up the support structures and to lay the tracks. You must plan the timing of the construction work carefully. A medium-sized wooden roller coaster takes about nine months to build. Because most amusement parks are open only during summer, you have the winter months to build the ride, but this time frame often means building in cold, wet weather.

Coaster Work

The DATA BOX on page 23 contains information about how long each part of the building work might take. Use this information to help you estimate the number of weeks it could take to complete all the jobs.

Be careful. Some time spans are given in weeks, and some are given in months. To convert weeks to months or months to weeks, think of one month as four weeks.

Math Challenge

Look at your answer to the COASTER WORK on page 22.

1) How many days will it take for all jobs to be completed?

2) Is your answer closest to
   a) 1 year?
   b) 1½ years?
   c) 2 years?

Stages of Construction

Here are some time estimates for the various stages of building a roller coaster. Some of these jobs can be done at the same time.

Survey

1 to 2 weeks to survey the building site and lay out the plan and position of the ride

Foundations

3 months for workers to dig the foundations for the ride

Structure

6 months to make the pieces of the coaster, take them to the site, build the structure, and tighten all the bolts

Tracks

2 to 3 months for a crew to stack layers of wood, cut the track, and add the track steel

Mechanical

4 weeks to install brakes and complete gate, chain, motor, and control systems

Coaster Fact

Sometimes, as a coaster is being built, parts of the design might be changed. On the Hades ride, both the approach to the lift hill and the end of the ride were changed well into the design process and after the turnaround for the ride had already been built.

TESTING AND TRIAL RUNS

When your roller coaster is complete, you must test it for safety. You need to be sure that the ride will pass the review of official safety inspectors. You might also want to do a trial run to make sure that the ride is exciting! You should do everything you can to make your roller coaster thrilling for riders. Now is also the time to decide how much to charge for a ride. If you set the cost too high, people might not go on the ride, but if you set it too low, you might not make enough money. Some theme parks simply charge an overall entrance fee. Then, each ride in the park is free!

Coaster Work

The DATA BOX on page 25 shows pictures of a roller coaster's support structure being built. The track support for a roller coaster may form a variety of shapes.

This sketch of part of a track support structure shows seven different shapes in seven different colors.

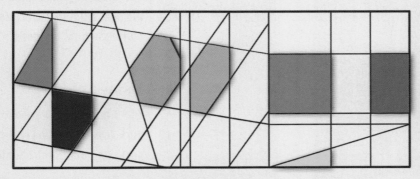

1) Can you name each of the shapes?
2) Which of the shapes have at least one right angle?

If you look closely, you can see the track of a roller coaster running around this theme park ride.

Built For Strength

These pictures show the support structure of a roller coaster being built. The triangle pattern provides maximum strength.

Math Challenge

Look at this picture.

How many equilateral triangles of different sizes do you see?

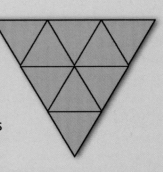

Before a roller coaster opens, safety inspectors carefully examine the ride. They look at how people will get on and off the coaster and make sure that safety precautions are taken while the ride is running. They pay particular attention to the restraints, usually lap bars or shoulder harnesses, that hold passengers inside the cars during the ride. Inspectors also may put height or age restrictions on a ride to keep small children out of danger. For many rides in the United States, passengers must be at least 48 inches tall. Congratulations! Your ride has passed the inspection. Your coaster is ready to roll!

Coaster Work

The DATA BOX on page 27 contains a graph
showing a rider's height above the ground
as a roller coaster moves along.
Use the graph to help you answer these questions.

1) How high above the ground is the rider after
   a) 1 second?
   b) 4 seconds?
   c) 9½ seconds?
   d) 5 seconds?

2) After about how many seconds is the rider at
   a) 150 feet?
   b) 10 feet?

3) The rider is 120 feet above the ground three times.
   How many times is the rider at a height of
   a) 150 feet?
   b) 115 feet?
   c) 90 feet?
   d) 30 feet?
   e) 13 feet?

The Inspector's Report

When inspectors examine roller coasters, they take lots of notes and measurements and make graphs that show a rider's height above the ground as the coaster moves along.

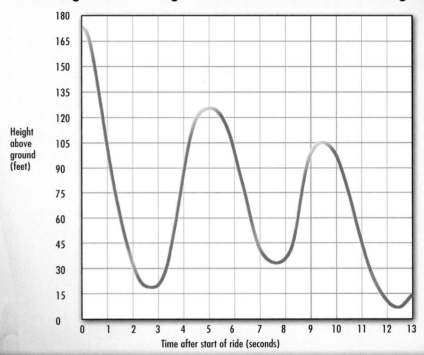

Height above ground (feet)

Time after start of ride (seconds)

Your roller coaster will give millions of people a thrilling experience!

Coaster Fact

You can tell whether people have enjoyed a ride by listening to what they say as they get off. People who build roller coasters say "The success of a ride can be measured in smiles."

Math Challenge

Use the graph in the DATA BOX above to help you answer these questions.

1) About how high is each of the graph's three hills?
2) How much lower is the second hill than the first hill?
3) How much lower is the third hill than the second hill?

MATH TIPS

PAGES 6–7

Coaster Work

TOP TIP: To find the number of years between two dates, subtract the older date from the newer date.

Example: 2003 – 1997 = 6 years

PAGES 8–9

Coaster Work

To use coordinates to find a point on a grid, read, first, along the bottom of the grid, then up the side.

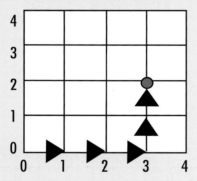

Example: For grid coordinates (3, 2), move 3 squares along the bottom, then 2 up to find the exact point.

Math Challenge

TOP TIP: To find the area of an irregular shape, count the number of whole squares inside the outline, then count the parts of squares. Buildings and other features inside the plot count as part of the area.

Example: The area of this shape = 6 squares.

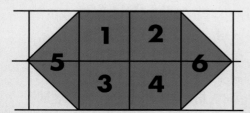

PAGES 10–11

Math Challenge

Here are two ways (methods) of multiplying by 2-digit numbers.

Example: 83 x 12

Method 1: Think of 12 as 1 ten and 2 ones.

STEP 1
Multiply by 2 ones (2).

```
  83
x 12
 166   2 x 83
```

STEP 1
Multiply by 1 ten (10).

```
  83
x 12
 166
 830   10 x 83
```

STEP 3
Add the products.

```
  83
x 12
 166
+830
 996
```

Method 2: Think of 83 x 12 as two problems.

```
  83              83        Add the products:   166
x  2    and     x 10                          + 830
 166             830                            996
```

PAGES 12–13

Math Challenge

Some fractions look different but actually stand for the same amount. All these fractions (*right*) have the same amount of the rectangle shaded. We say they are equivalent.

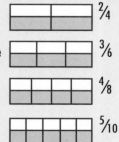

To make equivalent fractions, multiply or divide the top and bottom numbers by the same number.

Example: All of the fractions in this box are equivalent.

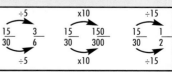

($\frac{1}{2}$ is the fraction in its simplest form because another fraction cannot be made with any smaller whole numbers on the top or the bottom.)

28

PAGES 14–15

Coaster Work

An angle is a measure of turn. Angles are measured in degrees. The symbol for degrees is °. One whole turn is 360°. It is called a complete revolution. A quarter turn is one-fourth of a complete revolution, which is 90°, or one right angle. There are four right angles in one whole turn.

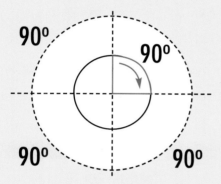

PAGES 16–17

Coaster Work

The perimeter of a shape is the distance all the way around its edge.

Math Challenge

To find a number that is exactly halfway between two other numbers, first, add the numbers together, then divide the answer in half (divide by 2).

Example: To find the number that is exactly halfway between 25 and 63, add 25 and 63.
$$(25 + 63 = 88)$$
Now divide the answer in half (divide by 2).
$$(88 \div 2 = 44)$$
So 44 is the number that is exactly halfway between 25 and 63.

PAGES 18–19

Coaster Work

To find out how many people can ride on each train, multiply the number of people per bench by the number of benches per car, and then multiply by the number of cars per train.

To find out how many rides a train can complete in one hour, remember that there are 60 minutes in one hour. Divide 60 minutes by the ride time for each train.

Math Challenge

To find how many people can go on each ride in one hour, multiply the number of people per train (the answers to Coaster Work question #1) by the number of rides per hour (the answers to Coaster Work question #3).

PAGES 22–23

Math Challenge

To change weeks into days multiply the number of weeks by 7.

Examples: 10 weeks = 70 days
20 weeks = 140 days
Remember that there are 365 days in one year (366 days in one leap year).

PAGES 24–25

Math Challenge

Try to be systematic when looking for the triangles. Start by counting the small triangles. Then look for larger triangles until you reach the largest triangle.

ANSWERS

PAGES 6-7

Coaster Work

1) a) Kingda Ka   3) The Ultimate and
   b) Kingda Ka   Tower of Terror
   c) Daidarasaurus
   d) Big Dipper

2) a) 344 feet   4) a) 5 years
   b) 328 feet   b) 12 years
   c) 216 feet   c) 82 years

Math Challenge

1) Kingda Ka   Hades
  Top Thrill Dragster The Beast
  Dodonpa   The Ultimate
  Tower of Terror   Daidarasaurus
  Millennium Force Big Dipper
  The Voyage

2) a) 6 coasters b) 1 coaster c) 3 coasters

PAGES 8-9

Coaster Work

1) a) Plot C b) Plot D c) Plot D d) Plot C
2) a) (3, 5) b) (1, 4) c) (6, 4) d) (0, 4)

Math Challenge

Area of plot A = 28 squares
Area of plot B = 15 squares
Area of plot C = 24 squares
Area of plot D = 17 squares

PAGES 10-11

Coaster Work

Designs 2 and 5 will work. In each of the other designs, another hill is larger than the lift hill.

Math Challenge

1) a) 75 feet   2) a) 900 inches
   b) 96 feet   b) 1,152 inches
   c) 75 feet   c) 900 inches

PAGES 12-13

Coaster Work

1) Plot D is a decagon. It has 10 sides.

2) triangle   quadrilateral

   pentagon   hexagon

   heptagon   octagon

   nonagon   decagon

Math Challenge

1) Fractions that are equivalent to $\frac{24}{36}$ include:
$\frac{2}{3}$, $\frac{6}{9}$, $\frac{12}{18}$, $\frac{48}{72}$, $\frac{240}{360}$, $\frac{2400}{3600}$, etc.

2) $\frac{2}{3}$

PAGES 14-15

Coaster Work

1) a) 720°   2) a) 8 right angles
   b) 1440°   b) 16 right angles
   c) 1080°   c) 12 right angles

Math Challenge

Size of turn	Fraction of a full turn	Fraction in its smallest form
a) 90°	$\frac{90}{360}$	$\frac{1}{4}$
b) 180°	$\frac{180}{360}$	$\frac{1}{2}$
c) 45°	$\frac{45}{360}$	$\frac{1}{8}$
d) 60°	$\frac{60}{360}$	$\frac{1}{6}$
e) 30°	$\frac{30}{360}$	$\frac{1}{12}$
f) 10°	$\frac{10}{360}$	$\frac{1}{36}$

PAGES 16-17

Coaster Work

1) 172 feet (inside) and 260 feet (outside)
2) 104 feet (inside) and 156 feet (outside)

PAGES 16–17

Math Challenge

Loop A: 216 feet
Loop B: 130 feet

PAGES 18–19

Coaster Work

1) Ride A carries 24 people per train.
Ride B carries 30 people per train.
Ride C carries 18 people per train.
So Ride B carries the most people per train.

2) Ride B   3) a) 20   b) 15   c) 30

Math Challenge

Ride A can carry 480 people.
Ride B can carry 450 people.
Ride C can carry 540 people.
So Ride C can carry the most people per hour.

PAGES 20–21

Coaster Work

1) a) one hundred forty-one feet
   b) one hundred seventy wooden coasters
   c) nine hundred legs
   d) one thousand two hundred ribbons
   e) four thousand seven hundred twenty-eight feet
   f) one thousand eight hundred eighty-two
      roller coasters
   g) one thousand seven hundred twelve
      steel coasters
   h) three thousand nine hundred items

2) a) 93   b) 308   c) 764   d) 1, 407   e) 2,020

Math Challenge

a) twenty
b) eight hundred
c) two
d) three thousand
e) seven thousand
f) fifty thousand
g) nine hundred thousand

PAGES 22–23

Coaster Work

Time estimate: 49 to 54 weeks

Math Challenge

1) 343 to 378 days
2) a) 1 year

PAGES 24–25

Coaster Work

1) isosceles
   triangle   heptagon

   square   pentagon

   hexagon   rectangle

   scalene triangle

2) The square, the scalene triangle, and the
   rectangle all have at least one right angle.

Math Challenge

9 small

3 medium-sized

1 large

Total: 13 equilateral triangles

PAGES 26–27

Coaster Work

1) a) 105 feet b) 90 feet c) 105 feet d) 125 feet
2) a) ½ second b) 12 seconds
3) a) once b) 3 times c) 5 times d) 3 times e) twice

Math Challenge

1) 173 feet (ft), 125 ft, 105 ft   2) 48 feet   3) 20 feet

31

GLOSSARY

AIRTIME the word that describes the butterflies-in-your-stomach, weightless feeling when a roller coaster car goes over a hill

BENTS the cross sections of the structure that supports a roller coaster's tracks. The metal bars used to make up the bents are called chords, diagonals, and legs.

BUNNY HOPS short, fun hills

CAMELBACK a roller-coaster hill that looks like the hump on a camel

CENTRIFUGAL FORCE the force that pushes something moving in a circle toward the outside edge of the circle

COORDINATES the points on a grid where two lines meet or intersect

CORKSCREW TURN a loop with a twist in it

CROSSOVERS the places where one section of a roller coaster crosses over or under another. As the ride hurtles toward a crossover, passengers think they are going to hit the ride's structure.

DOG LEG a type of out-and-back ride that turns partway along the layout

EQUILATERAL TRIANGLES triangles with all three sides of the same length

FRICTION a rubbing force that slows down a moving object

GRAVITY the force that draws objects downward toward the center of Earth

GRID a network of uniformly spaced horizontal and vertical lines

HORSESHOE TURN a U-shaped turn

HYDRAULIC having a mechanism that works by means of a moving liquid

ISOSCELES TRIANGLE a triangle with two sides that are the same length

LOOP the place where a roller coaster track makes a complete revolution, turning passengers completely upside down when the train is at the top of the loop

OUT AND BACK a ride that travels straight out, then turns around and comes back

PLOT MAP a simple drawing showing an area of land that is available for building a structure of some kind

PRETZEL a combination of half-loops and half-corkscrews that form the shape of a twisted pretzel

RESTRAINTS the bars, straps, or harnesses that hold passengers securely inside roller coaster cars during rides

RIBBONS thin metal bars that connect bents

SCALENE TRIANGLE a triangle that has all three sides of different lengths

STRUCTURE the framework or scaffolding that holds up a roller coaster. Both wooden and steel roller coasters can have metal structures.

TRAIN several roller coaster cars joined in a chain and traveling together as a single unit

Measurement Conversions

1 inch = 2.54 centimeters (cm)
1 foot = 0.3048 meter (m)
1 mile = 1.609 kilometers (km)
1 pound = 0.4536 kilograms (kg)